Confident Conversation

Overcoming Social Anxiety through Improved Communication

Table of Contents

Chapter 1. Introduction

In this empowering Special Report, we delve into the art of Confident Conversation: Overcoming Social Anxiety through Improved Communication. Isn't it fascinating how the simple act of converging words can transform lives? Imagine feeling that rush of confidence as you articulate your thoughts eloquently, beaming in the thrill of a lively discussion. No more clammy hands, no more awkward silences, all those fears stowed away in the past. You're poised to conquer the world, one conversation at a time. If you've ever felt your heart in your throat at the thought of a simple social interaction, this is the significant leap you've been waiting for. Dissecting the enigma of human communication, this formidable report is set to turn not just nervous talkers into eloquent speakers, but also transform shy turtles into social butterflies. Bursting with reliable research, practical tips and empowering strategies, this report is your guide to unlocking the door to confident engagements. Gear up for the metamorphosis!

Chapter 2. Understanding Social Anxiety

The ability to stand tall in a room, to converse freely and expressively, can feel like a magical power for those gripped by the icy fingers of social anxiety. The journey to understanding and ultimately overcoming social anxiety is one of introspection, discovery, and strategy.

2.1. Understanding the Specter of Social Anxiety

Social anxiety, also known as social phobia, signifies an intense fear or stress that people experience when facing social situations. This fear could be triggered by a variety of situations, from speaking in public, meeting new people, to even the simple act of eating in public.

Individuals suffering from social anxiety exhibit intense apprehension or fear of being negatively evaluated or judged by others. Often, this concern is so debilitating that it drastically curtails their ability to partake in various social settings, restricting personal growth and daily functioning.

2.2. Origins and Triggers: Where does Social Anxiety Come From?

The source of social anxiety is multifaceted, an intricate web of intertwined threads of biology, personal experiences, and learned behavior. Some people may have a heightened genetic predisposition to anxiety, implying a family history of social anxiety or related mental conditions. Brain structure, specifically the structure of the amygdala, has also been linked with social anxiety levels.

Beyond biology, personal experience plays a significant role in shaping one's susceptibility to social anxiety. The experiences in early life, especially those revolving around relationships with parents, other family members, or peers, significantly influence the development of social anxiety. Traumatic experiences like bullying, abuse, or neglect can leave enduring psychological scars.

In a world where we're continually compared and ranked, societal pressures and norms can also unearth social anxiety. Prevailing traditions that place outsized emphasis on approval, conformity, and perfection can set unrealistic expectations, engendering fear and nervousness in social settings when these lofty goals are unmet.

2.3. Behavioral and Physical Manifestations of Social Anxiety

The manifestations of social anxiety stretch far beyond the realms of psychological distress. No two people with social phobia experience it in the same way, but some physical and behavioral symptoms seem to be commonly shared.

Physical symptoms may include a rapid heart rate, queasiness or an upset stomach, a shaky voice, trembling hands or knees, profuse sweating, difficulty in breathing, dizziness, and hot or cold flashes.

Behaviorally, those with social anxiety may purposefully avoid situations where they feel they might be the center of attention. Others may grimace at the thought of being introduced to others, panic at the prospect of being watched or observed while doing something, or dread any social event where interaction might be unavoidable.

2.4. The Impact of Social Anxiety on Quality of Life

When left unchecked, social anxiety can cast a significant toll on the overall quality of life of an individual. It may affect relationships, both professional and personal, setting boundaries that limit the range of experiences one might have. It can also restrict career progress as people with social anxiety may find it challenging to partake in social work situations, like meetings or presentations.

Equally significant, social anxiety can lead to low self-esteem and heightened self-consciousness, affecting one's view of themselves and the world around them.

2.5. Breaking the Cycle and Owning Your Narrative

Understanding social anxiety helps establish the foundation for grappling effectively with its impacts. Clinical psychologists and psychiatrists provide professional support for diagnosing and dealing with such disorders. A range of therapeutic options exists, such as Cognitive Behavioral Therapy (CBT), exposure therapy, and certain pharmacological treatments, which may help alleviate the symptoms of social anxiety.

But therapy alone is not the panacea. Augmenting these treatments with self-help strategies, such as regular workouts, healthy sleep patterns, moderated caffeine and alcohol intake, and a balanced, nutritious diet can significantly amplify the effects of therapy.

Moreover, the power of human connection can be instrumental in managing social anxiety. Building a robust support system of friends, family, or others grappling with similar concerns might provide individuals with a safe space where they can share experiences, insights, and coping strategies.

In conclusion, understanding social anxiety is the first significant stride on the road to managing it. With realizations about the cause and impact of social anxiety, one is better prepared to envision a future where it no longer holds sway over every social interaction. After all, knowledge, as they say, is power, and in this case, it's the power to reclaim the narrative of your life and the confidence that comes with it.

Chapter 3. Decoding the Power of Conversation

Comprehending the phenomenon of conversation is like unraveling an intricate puzzle. At the surface, it may seem like a simple exchange of words and ideas. However, it encapsulates a whole range of elements, including body language, tone of voice, facial expressions, phrases, and figures of speech. Delving deeper into these facets will unlock the mysteries and sheer power conversation holds, leading you towards a more confident, eloquent, and impactful communication style.

3.1. Understanding Conversation Mechanics

Conversation, in essence, is a two-way street. The exchange of thoughts, ideas, and emotions is as much about listening as it is about speaking. A good conversationalist observes before responding, processes the spoken words, comprehends the unspoken cues, and crafts calculated yet organic responses. Mechanics is not about becoming a robotic orator - it's about understanding and utilizing the pillars of conversation for enhanced interaction.

Listening, absorbing information, responding appropriately, and signaling interest through non-verbal queues are the four cornerstones of conversation. Hone each of these aspects, and you're on your way to mastering the art of engaging communications.

3.2. The Role of Non-Verbal Communication

Often, what you don't say in a conversation bears as much weight as what you do. Non-verbal communication, including facial expressions, body language, and tone of voice, paints a comprehensive picture of your thoughts.

Take note of your body language: are you slumping, avoiding eye contact, or crossing arms in defensiveness? All of these could be projecting an image that's averse to open communication. Aim to maintain a relaxed posture, establish comfortable eye contact, and keep an inviting and open body language to encourage a more fruitful conversation.

Your tone of voice is another potent tool. A monotone voice can lead a lively conversation to an untimely demise, while unnecessary amplification might come off as aggressive rather than passionate. Experiment with pitches, inflections, and pauses. Work on mirroring the listener's tone to foster comfort and rapport, but remember to retain your individuality.

Leveraging non-verbal cues can help you steer the conversation, making you an effective communicator and a more active participant even when you're not the one speaking.

3.3. Harnessing the Power of Empathy

Empathy, the ability to understand and share the feelings of others, can be a game-changer in conversations. A good empath can gauge emotions, understand viewpoints, and respond appropriately. The psychic distance between the participants shrinks, fostering an environment of trust and understanding.

The likelihood of conflict decreases as empathetic responses pave the way for the mutual acceptance of perspectives. Practice active listening with the aim of empathizing with your conversation partner's viewpoint, even when countering their perspective. This will not only make your speech more engaging but also convey respect for their views.

3.4. Influencing Through Persuasive Speaking

Effective conversation isn't about directing or commanding - it's about influencing. Persuasive speaking, an art in itself, can completely transform the dynamics of your conversation. The goal is not to impose your ideas on others but to present them appealingly and convincingly.

Tools for persuasive speaking include storytelling, logical reasoning, citing statistics or evidence, appealing to the listener's emotions, etc. However, remember that credibility is critical. Be truthful to maintain the listeners' trust in your words.

Furthermore, strategic use of language - positive phrasings, strong action verbs, vocabulary that appeals to the senses - can help strengthen your persuasive powers.

3.5. The Art of Pacing and Pausing

Maintaining an appropriate pace is vital to keep the listener engaged. Too fast, and they might not absorb what you're saying; too slow, and they might lose interest. Being intentional about your speed of speaking will help you retain control of the conversation.

Strategic pauses can help add impact and depth to your words. A pause can give both you and your listener time to process the conversation and formulate responses. It can also emphasize points, control conversation dynamics, and ensure that your key messages are resonating with the listeners.

As you embark on your journey of mastering conversation and

overcoming social anxiety, remember that success lies in embracing your unique style. There are no hard and fast rules when it comes to communication: it's about finding what works for you. It's about blending knowledge, practice, and insightful experimentation to transform each conversation into an opportunity to connect, influence, and thrive. This is the magnificent power of conversation - now at your command!

Chapter 4. Symptoms and Causes of Social Anxiety

Social anxiety, often misunderstood as mere shyness or introversion, is a chronic mental health condition characterized by intense fear and avoidance of social situations. It significantly interferes with a person's daily functioning and overall well-being.

4.1. The Burden it Bears

According to the Social Anxiety Institute, social anxiety is the third largest mental health problem in the world today, crossing boundaries of race, age, and socioeconomic status. Far from a fleeting concern, social anxiety takes toll on a person's educational and occupational progress, peer relationships, and self-esteem. The effects are pervasive, affecting almost every aspect of the life of someone with the disorder.

4.2. Dissecting the Symptoms

While it's normal to feel nervous in some social situations, individuals with social anxiety disorder worry excessively about being judged or scrutinized by others. They may experience symptoms including rapid heart rate, trembling hands, dry mouth, blushing or sweating even in non-threatening scenarios. There's a constant feeling of being watched and evaluated by others. Over time, the fear may be generalized to almost all social situations, in severe cases, leading to isolation and withdrawal.

Symptoms can be broadly classified into three categories:

1. Physical symptoms: These may include blushing, fast heartbeat, trembling, sweating, upset stomach or nausea, trouble catching

your breath, dizziness or lightheadedness, and muscle tension.

2. Emotional symptoms: Excessive self-consciousness and anxiety in everyday social situations are stark signs of social anxiety. You might fear embarrassment and humiliation, and scrutinize your already mortifying actions in retrospect, only fuelling the tense cycle.

3. Behavioral symptoms: You may avoid social situations to a point where it disrupts your life. Severe stress may lead to withdrawing from situations where you may be the center of attention.

4.3. Tracing the Causes

The causes of social anxiety disorder can be traced back to a complex interplay of genetic, environmental, and psychological factors. While no "social anxiety gene" has been discovered, it is believed that individuals may have a genetic predisposition to develop the disorder, making it more likely in those who have a family history of mental health disorders.

Environmental factors, including upbringing and early life experiences, also contribute significantly. A history of bullying, abuse, or teasing, can make individuals more prone to social anxiety. Being brought up in an environment that overly emphasizes public image or appearance, or one that restricts social interaction, can also contribute.

Psychological factors involve aspects of self-perception and cognitive patterns. Individuals with social anxiety often carry a negative self-image and engage in negative self-talk. They also tend to misinterpret neutral or benign social cues as negative, leading to avoidant behavior and further enhancing their fears.

4.4. The Lurking Comorbidity

Interestingly, social anxiety is often accompanied by other mental health disorders. Comorbidity with depression is quite common, as feelings of isolation, low self-esteem, and avoidance may trigger depressive symptoms. It is also commonly seen in conjunction with other anxiety disorders, obsessive-compulsive disorder, and eating disorders. The combination of disorders poses unique challenges in diagnosis and treatment, calling for a comprehensive, multidisciplinary approach.

4.5. Spotting Social Anxiety in Children

Though it tends to surface during the teenage years, social anxiety can present itself in younger children as well. It's crucial to be aware of signs such as extreme shyness, fear of making mistakes, avoidance of school, crying or tantrums before social events, and even refusal to speak in specific situations (selective mutism). Early intervention can play a crucial role in preventing the escalation of symptoms and future struggles.

In conclusion, understanding the symptoms and causes of social anxiety is the first crucial step towards tackling it. With this foundation, we can explore various interventions and strategies to manage the disorder effectively. Remember, the goal is not just to alleviate the symptoms, but to enable individuals to engage confidently in social situations, to express themselves freely, and to live their lives to the fullest. The journey may be challenging, but it is certainly possible. And, ultimately, incredibly rewarding.

Chapter 5. Communication and Its Influence on Self-Esteem

Of all the skills that one can cultivate in the pursuit of personal development, communication holds a significant position. It's not only about transferring information. It's about understanding the emotion and intention behind that information.

5.1. Understanding Communication

To begin with, communication isn't solely what you speak. It encompasses a vast landscape including body language, tone of voice, facial expressions and even the silence between the words. It's a symphony, where each element complements and affects the other, creating a cascade of impressions.

When we interact more deeply with others, expressing our viewpoints, ideas, and feelings, we don't merely exchange words. We exchange parts of ourselves, our identities. In the receipt and understanding of this self-conveyance, we find validations of our existence, which essentially contributes to self-esteem.

5.2. Layers of Communication

Communication isn't simply about solving problems or exchanging information. It has layers that stretch far deeper. The late psychologist, Abraham Maslow classified human needs into a pyramid, where each level's fulfillment facilitates you to move on to the next. Communication parallels this pyramid in enhancing self-esteem at each stage.

Beginning with bottom-most physiological needs, communication helps humans to fulfill these needs, directing our path to survive. Going upwards, in safety needs, language and expression make it possible to establish rules and security, fostering a sense of safety. In the third layer of belonging and love needs, communication acts as the primary facilitator of relationships, allowing us to convey feelings and comprehend affection.

As we reach the fourth level, the esteem needs, communication comes into the light of admiration, self-worth and personal value. It's here that one begins to realize the significant effects of communication on self-esteem.

In the final apex - self-actualization, communication allows us to express and understand the unique attributes of ourselves, inspiring growth and self-realization.

5.3. Role of Active Listening

Contrary to popular belief, effective communication is not all about talking. Being an active listener is just as crucial, if not more, for fostering healthy communication. Active listening involves wholeheartedly focusing, understanding, responding, and then remembering what is being said.

Active listening provides feedback that validates the speaker, creating trust and connection. Its importance can't be overstressed in constructing self-esteem. To be heard and understood is a powerful validation that boosts one's self-perception and value.

5.4. Impact of Non-verbal Communication

Non-verbal cues such as body language, tone, gestures, and facial expression can often speak volumes more than the words themselves. Each smirk, frown, yawn, crossed arm, or relaxed posture adds a layer to the conversation, significantly impacting the perception others have of you and, in turn, your perception of yourself.

Learning to control and convey positive non-verbal signals can greatly enhance your communication skills, thereby impacting your self-esteem. Non-verbal communication cues are instrumental in showing confidence, friendliness and openness.

5.5. Language Selection: Self & Others

The choice of our words matters. Often, we undermine ourselves without even realizing it by our language choices. Phrases such as "I'm just going to..." or "I guess I could..." discount our efforts and create a negative image. You inevitably believe about yourself what you repeatedly say about yourself. Disparaging language results in disparagement of self-value.

Just as self-talk matters, language employed towards others greatly contributes to their self-esteem. Affirmative language fosters positivity, encouragement and an uplifting atmosphere. It contributes constructively to an individual's self-belief, fortifying their identity.

5.6. Growth of Confidence and Self-Esteem

Self-esteem is closely associated with self-confidence, and both undergo simultaneous growth when communication skills are improved. When you have far-reaching communication skills, you are likely to feel naturally confident.

This confidence, in turn, bolsters your self-esteem. You feel more connected with your surroundings, more recognized for your opinions and your ideas, more validated for your existence. With each successful communication, you leave an impression, a mark. With this realization comes the growing assurance of your worth.

5.7. Conclusion

Communication, by its most fundamental definition, is the act of connecting, of creating a bond, of creating understanding. As such, it is profoundly tied to our perception of self – our self-esteem. Understanding this powerful tool and mastering it holds the key to a robust sense of personal value and confidence.

In essence, effective communication fosters self-worth, enhances relationships, promotes authenticity, encourages self-actualization and galvanizes our integral growth – making us stronger, happier, and more resilient. Articulating thoughts clearly, listening actively, harnessing control over non-verbal cues, and employing positive language all contribute towards healthier self-esteem. Equipped with these skills, you'll notice a transformation in your interaction with others and with yourself.

For the person ready to overcome their social anxiety, this is the light at the end of the tunnel. It's your path to not only tackle conversations with elegance but also to view yourself in a new, positive light - a light that illuminates your inherent worth.

Chapter 6. Practical Strategies to Overcome Communication Anxiety

Starting off, the first point of significance to remember is that effective communication is not about perfection, but connection. This realization can be the key to mitigating those fear-induced hurdles that crop up, which tend to be unwarranted.

6.1. Understanding Communication Anxiety

Before diving into strategies for overcoming communication apprehension, it's essential to understand what it is and why it happens. Communication anxiety, often referred to as social anxiety or performance anxiety, is characterized by intense nervousness or fear about social interactions or situations involving speaking. It can manifest as a general fear of social situations, or it may be attached to specific situations such as public speaking, small group discussions, or even one-on-one conversations.

This type of anxiety often stems from a fear of judgment or negative evaluation by others. As social beings, humans are naturally inclined to seek acceptance and avoid rejection. When we perceive a social situation as threatening—such as worrying that we might say something embarrassing or not be able to articulate our thoughts well—we respond with anxiety.

Understanding this can provide a sense of comfort. It's natural and human to feel nervous about communication in certain situations. Yet it is important to recognize when this anxiety starts to interfere with our ability to express ourselves or results in avoiding social interactions altogether.

6.2. Identifying Your Triggers

Everyone experiences communication anxiety differently, and it's often linked to specific triggers. Understanding what situations or aspects of communication make you anxious is the first step to formulating an effective strategy for overcoming this fear. These triggers could be anything from speaking to new people, expressing a dissenting opinion, or even making small talk at a social event.

Unfortunately, there isn't a one-size-fits-all solution to this problem as communication anxiety varies greatly depending on individual factors such as personality, past experiences, and even cultural background. Hence, the first practical strategy recommended is self-investigation, identifying those precise instances when you feel the anxiety kicking in.

6.3. Building Self-Confidence

Self-confidence is a powerful antidote to communication anxiety. Building self-confidence involves becoming comfortable with oneself, recognizing personal strengths, and developing an inner belief that you can successfully communicate your thoughts and ideas. One way of building self-confidence is by focusing on your knowledge and skills.

Engage in activities that foster your intellectual growth and add to your knowledge bank. Remember, everyone has something valuable to bring to a conversation, and you're no exception. Another strategy that can be utilized is to maintain a list of your achievements, no matter how big or small they may seem. Regularly reflecting on these can boost your self-confidence and equip you better to tackle communication anxiety.

6.4. Practicing Mindfulness and Relaxation Techniques

When it comes to anxiety, it's all about coping – not escaping. Techniques like mindfulness, a type of meditation where you focus on being intensely aware of what you're sensing and feeling in the moment, without interpretation or judgment, can alleviate anxiety symptoms and promote relaxation.

Progressive muscle relaxation is another technique that involves tensing and then relaxing each muscle group. This practice aids in recognizing what tension—as a typical response to anxiety—feels like and understanding how to release it. Both these strategies can be instrumental tools in your anxiety management arsenal, ultimately helping to lessen communication anxiety.

6.5. Embracing Assertiveness

Being assertive is often misconstrued as being aggressive. However, it differs greatly. Assertiveness is about clearly expressing your thoughts and feelings while also respecting the thoughts and feelings of others. It's a balanced, respectful way of communication that can significantly reduce anxiety, as it brings the assurance of having expressed oneself effectively.

Practicing assertiveness can begin with small steps such as expressing your opinion during a conversation, setting personal boundaries, or learn to say no when required. Over time, as you grow more comfortable, this practice can profoundly boost your confidence and reduce communication anxiety.

6.6. Using Visualization Techniques

Visualization is a powerful technique, often used by athletes, speakers and performers, to improve performance. The idea is to create a vivid, successful image of the task at hand, so as to subconsciously boost confidence. In the context of communication, envisioning a successful conversation or presentation can help reduce anxiety. This goes a long way in prepping your mind for the actual event, eventually leading to its success.

As you can see, there is no single magic bullet for overcoming communication anxiety. It would certainly be beneficial to experiment with these strategies, to observe which ones are most effective for you. Remember, growing and refining your communication skills is a journey – one that's grounded in patience, practice and a positive mindset.

Perhaps, the most important thing to remember is that communication is not just about speaking but also about listening. Aim to cultivate not just speaking skills but also the art of active listening. When we focus on understanding others and their perspectives, we naturally let go of the anxiety of constantly evaluating what we're going to say next. Adding this practice to these practical strategies can provide a holistic approach to overcoming communication anxiety, priming you toward a more confident future in all your personal and professional interactions.

Remember, Rome wasn't built in a day, and neither will you be able to shrug off communication apprehension overnight; these things take time and a combination of strategies. With determination and practice, anyone can overcome their reservation and communicate confidently and effectively.

In conclusion, the transformative journey from suppressing fear to expressing words with confidence and ease is undeniably empowering. Be patient, stay mindful, dare to express, and get ready to unlock your potential with undeniable eloquence and newfound prowess. Step forth into the world, turning those conversations into riveting soliloquies that inspire and engage, unveiling the charismatic conversationalist in you. Buckle up for an exciting journey towards overcoming communication anxiety!

Chapter 7. Skills for Confident Conversation

Before we embark on this exploration towards confident conversation, it's important to remember that the path to eloquent speaking and effective communication is not a single giant leap; instead, it's a series of small steps, each contributing towards your growth, like pieces of a jigsaw puzzle. So here we go - let's start piecing this puzzle together!

7.1. Understanding your Fear

Let's first unravel this monster that stops you from expressing yourself: social fear. It's perfectly normal for anyone to feel nervous while speaking to unfamiliar people or even while addressing a familiar crowd. However, understanding why this fear grips you is key to overcoming it.

Acknowledge that your fear is your body's protective response. The unknown makes us uncomfortable, and our body responds by becoming hyper-aware and anxious. This is linked to our survival instincts. Embrace it, identify it for what it is, and ask yourself, "What's the worst that could happen?" Quantifying your fear often takes away its potency.

7.2. Body Language: The Unspoken Word

People communicate more through body language than they do verbally. This silent language can either augment or depreciate your verbal message. Thus, mastering body language is a vital part of confident conversation.

Let's start with our posture. A slouched back can make you appear unsure and weak. Conversely, standing straight with your shoulder blades pulled back exudes confidence. Practice this stance regularly until it becomes a part of you.

Eye contact is another major component. It displays attentiveness and respect. However, too much can be just as detrimental as too little. Therefore, balance is key. Typically, maintaining eye contact for about 60-70% of the conversation is a good rule of thumb.

Smiles are powerful. They can uplift your mood, and those of others around you. They convey a positive, approachable vibe. Remember to smile genuinely, though; forced smiles often have the reverse effect.

7.3. Listening Actively

Active listening is integral for confident and effective communication. By practicing active listening, you engage with the speaker, understand their perspective, and respond effectively. This involves being present in the moment, refraining from interruptions, and providing feedback or asking thoughtful questions when it's your turn to speak.

Verification is a useful tool within this. Repeat what you understood back to the speaker, to ensure you've comprehended it properly. This prevents any miscommunication and shows your commitment to the conversation.

7.4. Words and Voices Matter

Your voice can influence the impact of your words. Being mindful of your voice projection, tone, and pacing can aid you in becoming a confident speaker. Speak clearly with a strong but pleasant tone. Use a moderate pace, and avoid filling silence with 'um's and 'uh's.

Instead, use brief pauses to gather your thoughts, which also lends gravitas to your speech.

Your vocabulary speaks volumes about you. While it's important to use a varied and extensive vocabulary to convey your thoughts effectively, there's no need to pepper your conversation with fancy words. Clarity should be your primary goal.

7.5. Seeking Common Ground

One way to build the confidence to converse is to start with things you're familiar with. It's easier to speak on topics you're knowledgeable about. This way, you create a connection, fostering trust and respect.

Even when the topic is unfamiliar, be honest about it. You can always ask open-ended questions to learn more from the other person. Confidence isn't about always knowing the answer; it's about being unafraid to ask questions.

7.6. Nurturing Emotional Intelligence

Emotional intelligence plays a crucial role in effective communication. By understanding and managing your emotions and empathizing with others, you can navigate tricky conversations with ease.

Practice empathy by being in tune with the other person's feelings during the conversation. It will help you respond appropriately and perhaps offer the right support.

7.7. The Art of Small Talk

Small talk helps break the ice. It might not seem groundbreaking, yet it fosters relationships and opens doors for deeper conversations. The key is to keep it light and positive. It could be as simple as talking about the weather or the latest trending series.

Practice these skills one at a time, as Rome was not built in a day, nor will your confidence be. The process might be long, but the results are worth the patience and effort. Now, equipped with these tools, you're on your way to becoming a confident conversationalist!

Chapter 8. Real-world Scenario Breakdown

To truly grasp how to triumph over social anxiety and develop confident conversation skills, let's step into various scenarios. It's through these real-life interactions and situations that we can apply the strategies and tactics discussed.

8.1. The Dinner Party Introductions

There you are, standing at the entrance of the room, your friend who invited you is off mingling. You're faced with a sea of unfamiliar faces. Here's how you can avoid freezing and instead make a flourishing grand entrance:

1. Enter with Confidence: Lift your shoulders, stand tall and walk confidently into the room. Your body language speaks volumes before your words do. A research study conducted by Amy Cuddy at Harvard University found that adopting power poses increases feelings of confidence.

2. Make the first move: Approach people instead of waiting for them to come to you. Use open-ended questions to spark up conversations. A good starter might be "How do you know our host?" or "What brings you here tonight?".

Remember, everyone at the party is there for social interaction, and they will welcome your approach.

8.2. The Class Presentation

You've to present a 10-minutes talk on a subject. Here's what you can do:

1. Preparation: Know your topic thoroughly. The more knowledge you have on the subject, the more confident you will feel while speaking about it. Create clear slides that summarize your key points, if applicable.

2. Practice: Rehearse your presentation several times, focusing on keywords and maintaining a steady rhythm.

3. Connect with your audience: Casual eye contact, gestures, and a friendly tone can make your presentation interactive and compelling.

Most importantly, give yourself a pep talk. Tell yourself, you are well-prepared, knowledgeable, and capable of delivering a great presentation.

8.3. The Job Interview

It's natural to experience a surge of nerves when attending a job interview. The following are the key points to focus on:

1. Prepare: Research the company, job role, and make sure you understand what is expected.

2. Rehearse common interview questions and answers: This will help you articulate your responses calmly and confidently.

3. Breathe: Use deep-breathing techniques to overcome nerves. This will help you calm and clear your mind.

Remember that the interviewer is a human too. They understand you might be nervous, and that's okay. Show them that even though you're anxious, you're capable of handling the job role.

8.4. The Social Networking Event

Professional networking can seem daunting, especially when you feel like a small fish in a big pond. Employ these tactics to navigate with confidence:

1. Listen More than you Speak: People appreciate good listeners. Show genuine interest in their conversation, respond appropriately, and relate it back to your experiences when necessary.

2. Have your 'Elevator Pitch' Ready: This brief, persuasive speech should explain who you are, what you do, and what kind of role you're looking for.

3. Ask for introductions: If you know someone at the event, ask them to introduce you to others. This can help put you at ease and make the process less overwhelming.

No matter the situation, there's a common thread running through each - preparation, practice, and genuine engagement. Arm yourself with a positive mindset and self-assured demeanor, and you're paving the way for confident engagements at every turn of life's journey. This real-world scenario breakdown should serve as a reliable model as you apply these principles in your day-to-day interactions and confront social anxiety with an armor of eloquence, eloquence that turns heads and commands attention. Self-assured interaction is but a conversation away.

Chapter 9. Cultivating Positivity and Self-Compassion

Mastering the art of confident conversation begins from within. It springs from a reservoir of positivity and is cemented by self-compassion. By cultivating these two essential qualities, we not only begin to view ourselves in a more positive light, but we also create an environment that boosts our communication skills.

9.1. The Power of Positive Thinking

Positive thinking is more than just having a good mood; it's a mental and emotional attitude that focuses on the bright side of life and expects positive results. It's a mindset that shifts the focus from problems to solutions, from failure to success, and from negativity to positivity.

Being positive starts by maintaining a list of positive affirmations handy that you can repeat to yourself. These affirmations are personal positive statements that affirm you're accepting, competent, and deserving.

Here's how to create a personal positive affirmation list:

1. Start by acknowledging the areas in which you lack confidence and then turn it around. For instance, "I am always becoming better at speaking to new people."

2. Make these affirmations specific and tangible.

3. Repeat these positive affirmations every day.

Over time, keeping this positive narrative can serve to override the negative self-talk you might usually entertain.

9.2. The Science of Optimism

Countless studies show that optimists are happier, healthier, and more successful than those who entertain a pessimistic attitude. Optimism has been linked to lower levels of depression, greater resistance to diseases, and even longer lifespan. This shows us that by being optimistic, you are not only creating a positive atmosphere for yourself but also paving the way for improved physical health.

To cultivate optimism, try these:

1. Keep a gratitude journal. Every day, list at least three things you're grateful for.

2. Surround yourself with positive influences.

3. Practice mindfulness. It helps you stay rooted to the present moment, instead of worrying about past failures or future challenges.

9.3. Self-Compassion: The Art of Being Kind to Yourself

Self-compassion goes hand-in-hand with positivity. It is all about accepting oneself and understanding that it's okay to make mistakes, instead of being overly self-critical. Just as we show compassion towards others, it's equally, if not more important, to be kind to ourselves.

Practicing self-compassion involves three core components:

1. Self-kindness versus self-judgment

2. Humanity versus isolation

3. Mindfulness versus over-identification

Practicing self-kindness means being supportive and understanding toward ourselves when we fail or make mistakes, rather than being harshly self-critical. Recognizing our common humanity involves acknowledging that all humans are imperfect, make mistakes, and everyone has these experiences, we don't have to feel isolated. Being mindful allows us to keep our personal issues in a balanced perspective, rather than exaggerating it or ignoring it.

9.4. Habits to Cultivate Self-Compassion

To foster a genuine sense of self-compassion, we must first recognize our thought patterns and then consciously work on altering them. Here are ways to incorporate self-compassion into your everyday routine:

1. Practice mindfulness even in small, everyday tasks. This could be as simple as appreciating the tangy burst of a tangerine or losing yourself in melody, flowing through your earphones.

2. Use a journal to write down instances where you've been unnecessarily hard on yourself. Observe the pattern, recognize it, and choose to respond differently.

3. Dedicate specific moments each day to focus solely on self-compassion. It could be a few minutes of affirmations or a self-kindness meditation.

4. When you find yourself wrestling with feelings of inadequacy, remind yourself that failure is part of the human condition.

9.5. Conclusion

Unlocking self-confidence and transforming social anxiety into insightful, lively conversations takes work and dedication. Cultivating positivity and self-compassion can be instrumental in overcoming fears and doubts that often hinder us from expressing ourselves fully. By staying positive, viewing the world through an optimistic lens, and accepting ourselves, we can shore up our self-confidence and face any social scenario with ease.

Chapter 10. Sustaining Confidence in Long-Term Conversations

In order to gain proficiency in the realm of confident conversation, it is crucial to master not only the art of initiating conversation but also maintaining that vigor throughout. Especially when it comes to long-term dialogues, the ability to keep the flame of your confidence burning brightly can become a daunting task. However, fret not! The following strategies will guide you to not only sustain your assurance, but also flourish in the process of engaging extensively with others.

10.1. Understanding the Importance of Consistency

The key ingredient in sustained confidence is consistency. Ensure that your conversational ethos remains unwavering even when the dialogue extends over considerable durations. Like the diligent sculptor shaping clay, you have to mold each conversation with the same degree of interest and enthusiasm, regardless of whether you've been speaking for five minutes or one hour.

Grasping the potency of steady communication might not seem like a massive leap, and often, individuals tend to overlook it. Yet, it is, without a doubt, one of the most influential factors and a testament to your assertions' credibility. Developing steady habits in your conversation flow could potentially create a ripple effect, enabling you to emerge triumphantly in the long run.

10.2. Equipping with the Power of Knowledge

An informed speaker is an influential speaker. By equipping yourself with a wealth of knowledge, you not only garner the potential to touch upon vast topics but also maintain the profundity of sustained discussions. Regular reading habits, coupled with an innate curiosity about the world, automatically nourishes your repository of conversational topics. As a result, you end up with myriad ammunition to sustain a dialogue, infusing it with facts and anecdotes throughout.

Moreover, extending this practice to understand the person you are conversing with can prove equally advantageous. Detailed awareness about their interests and viewpoints sets you at a vantage point in the dialogue, enabling you to steer it in directions that would engage them profoundly.

10.3. Embracing the Silence

As counterintuitive as it may seem, embracing the silence is a powerful tool in maintaining your conversational confidence. This valuable pause allows you to gather your thoughts, frame the language, and assess the conversation thus far.

An eloquent speaker utilizes periods of silence as punctuation in their verbal narrative, providing the listener with a moment to absorb what's been said. Far from being an awkward break in dialogue, these tranquil interludes can be the gateway to deeper, more meaningful exchanges.

10.4. The Art of Constructive Listening

Listening is, without a doubt, one of the most influential elements of a conversation. Yet, its constructive variant takes this a level higher. This involves the active engagement of your cognitive abilities, comprehending cues from the speaker's narrative, asking clarifying questions, summarizing shared thoughts, and demonstrating empathy.

Constructive listening provides the necessary support in the conversational journey, navigating both parties through the subtle nuances of intimacy and understanding. By mastering this crucial skill, you can enhance the duration and depth of your conversations, strengthening your confidence and credibility in the process.

10.5. Successfully Incorporating Humor

Infusing humor into your dialogue is a potent confidence booster. The ability to laugh and make others laugh not only lightens the conversational ambience but also solidifies bonds between individuals. The resulting comfort and relaxation pave the way for longer, more enjoyable discussions. Moreover, humor serves as a fantastic buffer against potential conversational stagnation, effectively breaking the ice and keeping the dialogue buoyant.

10.6. Feedback: A Crucial Support Pillar

One should never underestimate the power of constructive feedback as a means to boost your own conversational confidence. By soliciting feedback, you engage in an active process of introspection and improvement. This aids in understanding where your strength lies and where you can further improve, thereby enhancing your effectiveness in sustaining long-term conversations.

10.7. Adapt, Adopt, and Improve

Finally, keep in mind that successful communication requires adaptability. Consider each conversation as a learning opportunity, a chance to adopt new strategies, refine your strengths, and work on areas of improvement. Confidence, while being a quality, is also a skill that you can harness and improve over time with practice and patience.

This journey might be marked with inevitable challenges and stumbling blocks. Remember, the goal is not perfection but progress. You're not aiming to become the most amazing conversationalist overnight. It is a process, and every small effort contributes positively towards enhancing your communication and boosting your confidence.

In conclusion, sustaining confidence in long-term conversations is a craft. It requires painstaking dedication and purposeful practice. But the results are nothing short of magical. Watch as doors of opportunity swing open, acquaintances evolve into friendships, and dialogues transform into dynamic exchanges of ideas. So gird up, step into this exciting journey of discovery and self-improvement, and let your confidence drive your conversations!

Chapter 11. Returning to the Social Arena: The Capsule of Transformation

Society is a diverse potpourri of opinions, perspectives, and identities. Here lies the potential for a thriving ecosystem of dynamic, diverse conversations. However, for those grappling with social anxiety, this beautiful palette of varying hues can appear intimidating or overwhelming. In this chapter, we will guide you to metamorphose your view, bestowing upon you the tools to gleefully stride into the social sphere with confidence and assuredness. So, let's dive head-first into what we call a 'Capsule of Transformation'.

11.1. Understand Your Fear

Before we learn to fight the dragon, we must first know the beast we are up against. Fear is not a monolith; it has many faces, forms and origins. Get a comprehensive understanding of your unique social anxiety. Does it stem from a fear of judgement or rejection, or the terror of slipping up during conversation, thereby attracting unwanted attention? Is your anxiety born of past experiences or does it lie rooted in introversion? Recognize and accept your fear - this acceptance is the first crucial step toward conquering any apprehension.

11.2. Embrace Imperfections

Perfection is an unrealistic ideal. Instead, accepting imperfections can be liberating. Slip-ups, stutters, or even small moments of awkwardness are part of being human. By letting go of the pursuit of an elusive 'perfect interaction', you allow room for organic, meaningful bonds to bloom. Remember, it's about connection, not perfection.

11.3. Develop Resilience

Resilience isn't an inbuilt quality; it's a learned and practiced habit. If a conversation doesn't go as planned, remember, it doesn't define you as a person. Learn to pick yourself up and dust off any emotional residue. Negative experiences should be learning curves, not life sentences. You can cultivate resilience by identifying and reframing negative thoughts, practicing self-compassion, and honing problem-solving skills. A confident conversationalist is not the one who never stumbles, but the one who gets up each time he falls.

11.4. Body Language And Confidence

Non-verbal cues contribute to a substantial part of human communication. Maintaining an open posture, making relaxed eye contact, and using natural gestures can convey confidence and approachability.

Practise this in front of a mirror or record yourself to observe and improve your body language. Notice if you're folding your arms, avoiding eye contact, or making small, self-soothing gestures that may portray anxiety.

11.5. Conversational Skills

Understanding the dynamics and the art of conversing is invaluable. Practice active listening. This doesn't merely involve hearing words; it's about understanding the emotional undertones, the perspectives and the motivations behind the words. Recapitulate or ask questions to show engagement and develop an equal, balanced interaction. Learn to balance speaking and listening. Aim for 'dialogue' rather than 'monologue'.

11.6. Expanding Your Comfort Zone

Taking small steps towards expanding your comfort zone can lead to significant results. Start by challenging yourself to engage in simple social interactions and gradually increase the complexity. With each interaction, you're pushing the boundaries of your comfort zone, emboldening yourself for more challenging situations.

11.7. Mindful Techniques

Research has established the effectiveness of mindfulness in managing anxiety. Mindfulness helps by anchoring you to the present, removing the disturbing influence of past embarrassments or future anxieties. Simple techniques like focusing on your breath, grounding yourself by paying attention to your senses, or practicing guided mindfulness meditations can significantly reduce anxiety.

11.8. Conclusion: The Voyage Of Transformation

The path towards confident conversation is not linear. It's a journey marked with challenges, obstacles, and small victories. It's essential to remember that the objective of this transformation is not to become someone else; instead, it's to become the best, most confident version of yourself. Your ability to communicate confidently should amplify your unique personality, beliefs, and perspectives, not shroud them.

Embrace this journey with patience, persistence, and positivity. Overcoming social anxiety and becoming a confident conversationalist is much more than a target. It's a voyage of personal growth, self-discovery, and ultimately, transformation.

Remember, each small step you take is a giant leap towards becoming a social butterfly, basking in the radiant hues of the social arena. Stay strong, stay relentless. The world awaits your symphony of words.

www.ingramcontent.com/pod-product-compliance
Lightning Source LLC
Chambersburg PA
CBHW070742260726
48660CB00007B/2943